Abkhazia is something of a paradox: a country that exists, in the physical sense of the word (a territory with borders, a government, a flag, a language), yet it has no legal existence because for almost twenty years it was not recognized by any other nation state. And so Abkhazia exists without existing, caught in a liminal space, a space in between realities. Which is why my first letter to Max was something of a message in a bottle thrown at sea. EB

Eric Baudelaire
4 bis Avenue de Line #304
75019 Paris, France

Maxim Gvinjia
Chamber of Commerce TPP
Confederats St 37
384900 Sukhum
REPUBLIQUE D'ABKHAZIE

By air mail
Par avion

Paris, June 29th 2012

Dear Max,

Are you there?

Eric

Maxim Gvinjia
Chamber of Commerce TPP
384900 Confederatov St. 37
Sukhum
République d'Abkhazie

Via Georgie

By air mail
Par avion

Paris, September 19th 2012

Dear Max,

Did you get this letter too? How is that possible?

I was sure it would come back to me... Imagine the post office worker in Paris, looking at a map, trying to figure out what to do with this letter. What route did it travel? What countries did it pass through? Who are these people along the way who figured out how to get it to you? What are their names?

Eric

LA POSTE 25658A
FRANCE 22-09-12

Maxim Gvinjia
Chamber of Commerce TPP
384900 Confederatov St. 37
Sukhum
République d'Abkhazie

By air mail
Par avion

Paris, September 20th 2012

Dear Max,

I haven't received a letter back from you. It's been almost 3 months. Does that mean the mail only circulates in one direction, from me to you, not the other way around? It's a bit of a one sided correspondence then, isn't it?

It's been a long time, Max! So much has happened. So much to catch up about. Do you still go up to the belvedere above the city, the ruined kiosk with a panorama of the bay? What's the view like from up there these days? Could you record some sounds next time you go?

Eric

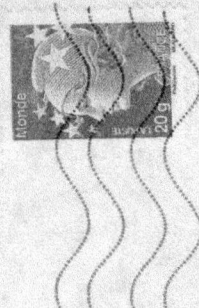

LA POSTE 256588
FRANCE 23-09-12

ZURÜCK PLZ: CN 15
RETURN

Maxim Gvinjia
Chamber of Commerce TPP
384900 Confederatov St. 37
Sukhum
République d'Abkhazie

R. ARMENIE

By air mail
Par avion

Nicht angenommen / Refused
Abgabestelle unbenutzt / Delivery point unused
Verstorben / Deceased
Anschrift ungenügend / Incomplete address
Unbekannt / Unknown
Verzogen / Moved
Falscher PLZ / Wrong zip code
Nicht behoben / Unclaimed

Rücksendedatum:
Return date:

LA POSTE 25658A
FRANCE 24-09-12

Maxim Gvinjia
Chamber of Commerce TPP
384900 Confederatov St. 37
Sukhum
République d'Abkhazie

By air mail
Par avion

Paris, September 23rd 2012

Dear Max,

Suits and ties, or jeans and t-shirts?

I guess you had a driver when you were minister of foreign affairs. What about now? Do you drive, or is it like the old days, catching rides with friends?

Eric

LA POSTE   25558A

FRANCE   25-09-12

Maxim Gvinjia
Chamber of Commerce TPP
384900 Confederatov St. 37
Sukhum
République d'Abkhazie

By air mail
Par avion

Paris, September 24th 2012

Dear Max,

How does it feel to be talking into a recorder?

It's strange to ask questions without hearing your answers... I guess I won't know until we're finished, will I?

Eric

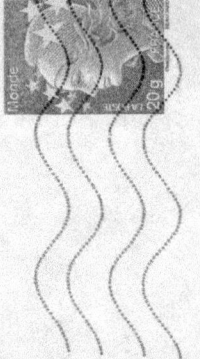

LA POSTE   26658A
FRANCE   26-09-12

Maxim Gvinjia
Chamber of Commerce TPP
384900 Confederatov St. 37
Sukhum
République d'Abkhazie

By air mail
Par avion

Paris, September 25th 2012

Dear Max,

It feels like I'm starting over again, a third attempt to tell this story.

The first time was 12 years ago. I took pictures, thousands of pictures. In black and white. I was never able to convince anybody to do anything with them. They're still sitting in a box somewhere, and if it weren't for nostalgia, I'd have thrown them away a long time ago.

The second time was in 2004 and 2005. I came back to see you, this time with a tripod, a big view-camera and color film. I made less pictures, a few hundred, and I printed some of them. I printed them really big.

Almost from the beginning, we said we'd make a film together. It seemed obvious that's where we were heading. So here we are Max.

Where do we start?

Eric

LA POSTE 25658A
FRANCE 28-09-12

Maxim Gvinjia
Chamber of Commerce TPP
384900 Confederatov St. 37
Sukhum
République d'Abkhazie

By air mail
Par avion

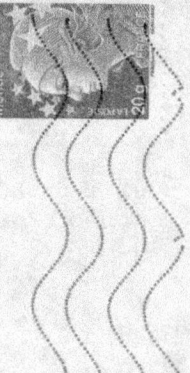

LA POSTE 256584

FRANCE 02-10-12

Maxim Gvinjia
Chamber of Commerce TPP
384900 Confederatov St. 37
Sukhum
République d'Abkhazie

By air mail
Par avion

Paris, October 1st 2012

Dear Max,

I distinctly remember not knowing what to photograph on that first trip. I was really at a loss, scratching my head about what to take pictures of.

I remember we mostly did a lot of talking. We had meetings with all kinds of officials from the government. We asked questions, but we didn't always feel we were learning much from the answers.

What did you think Dov and I had come for? What did you think we wanted?

Eric

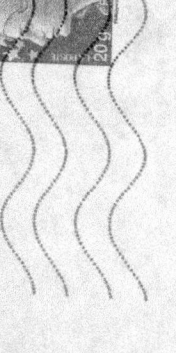

LA POSTE 25658A

FRANCE 05-10-12

Maxim Gvinjia
Chamber of Commerce TPP
384900 Confederatov St. 37
Sukhum
République d'Abkhazie

By air mail
Par avion

Paris, October 3rd 2012

Dear Max,

Your father disappeared at the beginning of the war. The rest of your family was safe. Would you like to talk about that? Or is it too personal?

Eric

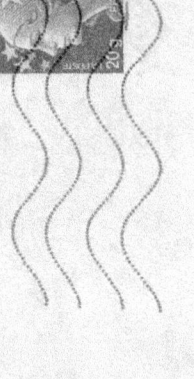

LA POSTE 25658A
FRANCE 09-10-12

Maxim Gvinjia
Chamber of Commerce TPP
384900 Confederatov St. 37
Sukhum
République d'Abkhazie

By air mail
Par avion

Paris, October 4th 2012

Dear Max,

I would really like to hear the story about your parents and the airplane kidnapping. I love that story.

Eric

PS: did you kidnap your wife, Max?

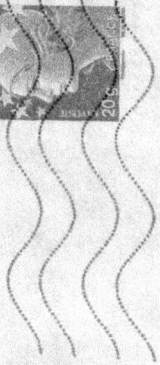

LA POSTE   256584

FRANCE   09-10-12

Maxim Gvinjia
Chamber of Commerce TPP
384900 Confederatov St. 37
Sukhum
République d'Abkhazie

By air mail
Par avion

Paris, October 9th 2012

Dear Max,

What does a diplomat for a country that isn't recognized do when he comes to the office in the morning?

Eric

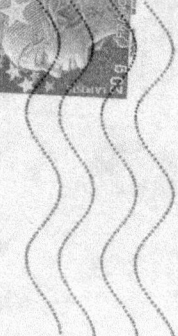

LA POSTE 25658A
FRANCE 10-10-12

Maxim Gvinjia
Chamber of Commerce TPP
384900 Confederatov St. 37
Sukhum
République d'Abkhazie

By air mail
Par avion

Paris, October 10th 2012

Dear Max,

How did it feel to be faced with non-recognition?

What does this word mean to you, recognition?

Eric

PS: I looked up "recognize" in the hip-hop dictionary, it says: "to respect; give honor by public acknowledgement."

LA POSTE 25558A

FRANCE 11-10-12

Maxim Gvinjia
Chamber of Commerce TPP
384900 Confederatov St. 37
Sukhum
République d'Abkhazie

Via GEORGIE

By air mail
Par avion

Paris, October 11th 2012

Dear Max,

Are there countries you don't recognize?

Eric

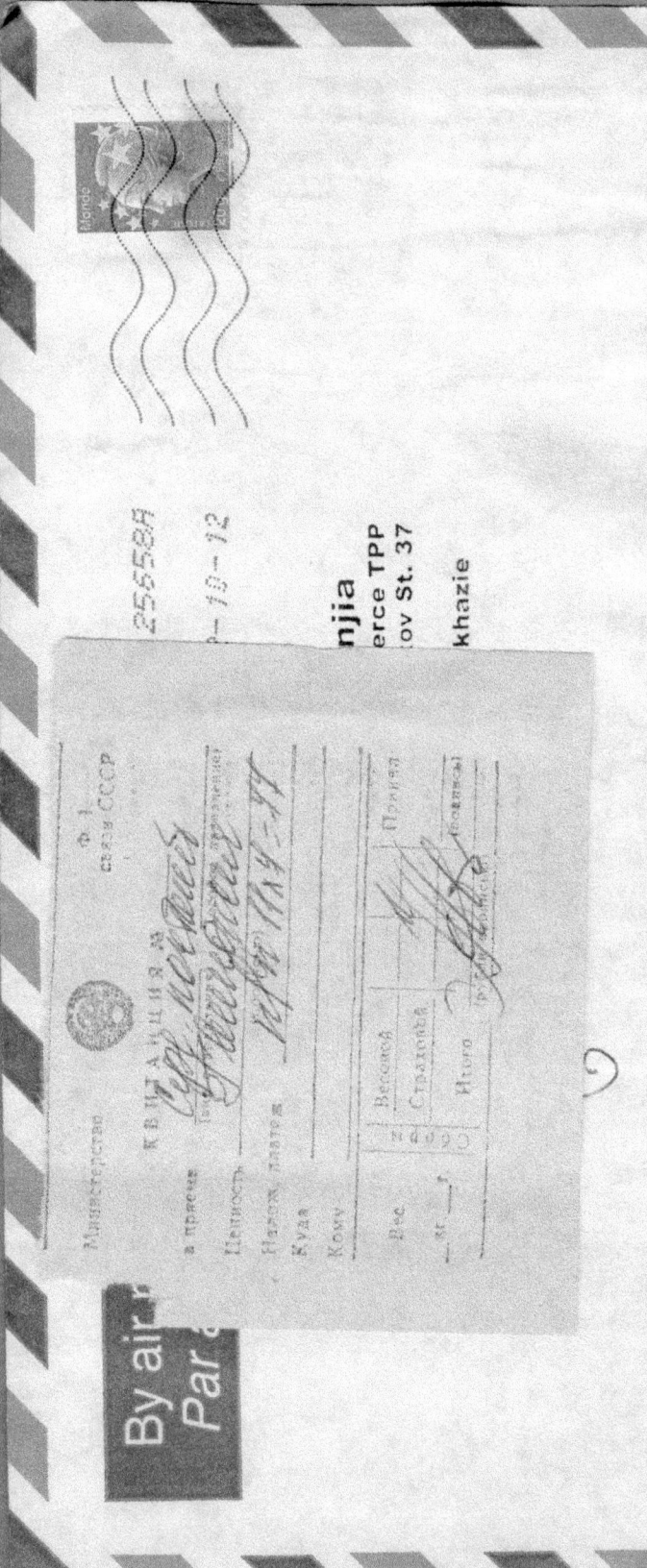

25558A
...-10-12

...njia
...erce TPP
...ov St. 37
...khazie

By air
Par

Paris, October 12th 2012

Dear Max,

I've been asking you a lot of questions about recognition, which means talking about how the other regards you. Perhaps the reverse consideration is more important: the way you regard yourself. And by "you" I mean the people of Abkhazia.

In the literature about nations a few ideas keep coming back. One of them is the idea that the state is imagined. It is the result of a collective imagination.

You, Max, always struck me as somebody for whom imagination is essential, not just in a political sense, but in the way you live your life in general. What did becoming a state mean for you? Was it important? What did you imagine?

Eric

LA POSTE   256538A
FRANCE   13-10-12

Maxim Gvinjia
Chamber of Commerce TPP
384900 Confederatov St. 37
Sukhum
République d'Abkhazie

Via GEORGIE

By air mail
Par avion

Paris, October 13th 2012

Dear Max,

Is a state something you build? Or was it always there?

Eric

LA POSTE 25658A
FRANCE 15-10-12

Maxim Gvinjia
Chamber of Commerce TPP
384900 Confederatov St. 37
Sukhum
République d'Abkhazie

By air mail
Par avion

Paris, October 14th 2012

Dear Max,

What does a state include? What does it exclude?

Eric

LA POSTE 256584

FRANCE 15-10-12

Maxim Gvinjia
Chamber of Commerce TPP
384900 Confederatov St. 37
Sukhum
République d'Abkhazie

Via Georgia

By air mail
Par avion

Paris, October 15th 2012

Dear Max,

Am I asking you the right questions?

If our roles were reversed, what would you ask me?

Eric

LA POSTE   256589

FRANCE   22-10-12

Ф.1
связи СССР

КВИТАНЦИЯ №

Министерство

в приеме
Ценность
Налож. платеж
У чем
Кому

Весовой
Страховой
Итого

By air mail
Par avion

Paris, October 20^h 2012

Dear Max,

I took pictures of landscapes. Empty landscapes. I remember thinking: here is a space that doesn't exist politically, and yet here I am photographing it. How is that possible? How can I be making a picture of a space that doesn't exist on the map? What is it that we see in those pictures?

Eric

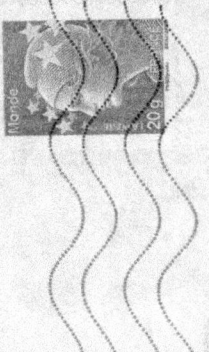

LA POSTE   256588
FRANCE   26-10-12

Maxim Gvinjia
Chamber of Commerce TPP
384900 Confederatov St. 37
Sukhum
République d'Abkhazie

By air mail
Par avion

Paris, October 25th 2012

Dear Max,

What can an image tell us about Abkhazia?

Eric

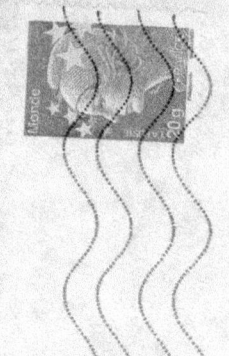

LA POSTE   256588A

FRANCE   26-10-12

Maxim Gvinjia
Chamber of Commerce TPP
384900 Confederatov St. 37
Sukhum
République d'Abkhazie

By air mail
Par avion

Paris, October 26th 2012

Dear Max,

What can an image tell us about imagination?

Eric

LA POSTE 256588
FRANCE 29-10-12

Maxim Gvinjia
Chamber of Commerce TPP
384900 Confederatov St. 37
Sukhum
République d'Abkhazie

By air mail
Par avion

Paris, October 29th 2012

Dear Max,

I wonder if you are still getting my letters. I wonder if they are arriving to you in the same order as I sent them. Is there even an order, Max?

Eric

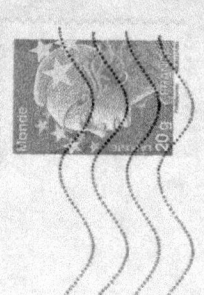

LA POSTE 256584
FRANCE 31-10-12

Maxim Gvinjia
Chamber of Commerce TPP
384900 Confederatov St. 37
Sukhum
République d'Abkhazie

By air mail
Par avion

Paris, October 30th 2012

Dear Max,

Once this correspondence has ended, I will come back to Abkhazia in the spring. This time I will have a film camera instead of a still camera.

So, what should I film, Max? What images should I make? Tell me a few things, a few places, I should shoot.

Eric

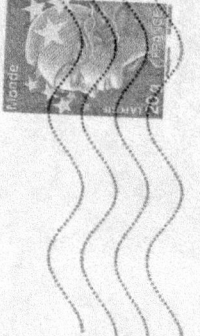

LA POSTE 256584
FRANCE 02-11-12

Maxim Gvinjia
Chamber of Commerce TPP
384900 Confederatov St. 37
Sukhum
République d'Abkhazie

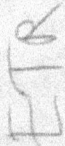

By air mail
Par avion

Paris, October 31st 2012

Dear Max,

What do you think these new images will reveal?

What will these images not reveal?

How will the film be different from the photographs I made during all those years?

Eric

Maxim Gvinjia
Chamber of Commerce TPP
384900 Confederatov St. 37
Sukhum
République d'Abkhazie

By air mail
Par avion

Paris, November 2nd 2012

Dear Max,

Are we making a documentary or a fiction?

Have we become characters in this film?

What roles should we play?

Eric

LA POSTE 255588
FRANCE 08-11-12

Maxim Gvinjia
Chamber of Commerce TPP
384900 Confederatov St. 37
Sukhum
République d'Abkhazie

Via Georgia

By air mail
Par avion

Paris, November 5th 2012

Dear Max,

Are we making a film that goes backward in time?

Are we making a film about memories?

Are we making a film about the future?

Eric

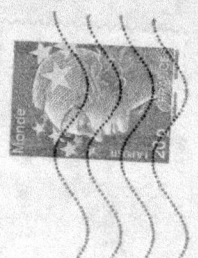

LA POSTE 25658A
FRANCE 09-11-12

Maxim Gvinjia
Chamber of Commerce TPP
384900 Confederatov St. 37
Sukhum
République d'Abkhazie

Via GEORGIE

By air mail
Par avion

Paris, November 6th 2012

Dear Max,

Are there any memories that should remain lost?

Should anything remain unsaid? Are there things I shouldn't film?

Eric

LA POSTE 25658A
FRANCE 10-11-12

Maxim Gvinjia
Chamber of Commerce TPP
384900 Confederatov St. 37
Sukhum
République d'Abkhazie

GÉORGIE

By air mail
Par avion

Paris, November 8th 2012

Dear Max,

We've talked about memory, and we've talked about imagination. I think what I'm trying to get to now is related to forgetting. It's possible that nations are based as much on what the people jointly forget as what they remember. That's why I need to ask you a different kind of question. I need to ask you about Georgians.

We can't make a film about Abkhazia and not address the question of Georgians, those who lived in Abkhazia for generations, grew up in Abkhazia, and left when the Georgian army lost the war. Many of these people haven't been able to return since the war.

Does building Abkhazia mean forgetting them?

Eric

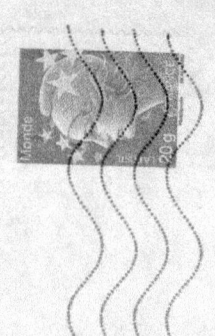

LA POSTE 256584
FRANCE 10-11-12

Maxim Gvinjia
Chamber of Commerce TPP
384900 Confederatov St. 37
Sukhum
République d'Abkhazie

Via GEORGE

By air mail
Par avion

Paris, November 9th 2012

Dear Max,

There are many ways to answer the question I asked you in my last letter. There are official answers, diplomatic answers, evasive answers but no simple answers, and no objective answers. I do not know which path you chose. I am not sure how we can raise this question together in the film we are making.

Perhaps we should try this: imagine a young Georgian man, a man your age, born in Abkhazia, who left during the war, and who hasn't been back: what do you think it would feel like for him to see this film? What would it feel like to see images of landscapes he knew as a child before the war, and cannot experience today?

Eric

LA POSTE 256658A
FRANCE 12-11-12

Maxim Gvinjia
Chamber of Commerce TPP
384900 Confederatov St. 37
Sukhum
République d'Abkhazie

Via GEORGIE

By air mail
Par avion

Paris, November 10th 2012

Dear Max,

Perhaps it's unfair of me to decide to make a film with a single voice, yours, and then ask you to represent another perspective, to speak for a hypothetical Georgian whose voice is absent from this film.

Perhaps I should let the camera speak instead of you. Search the landscape for images that will speak of absence. Can we let images replace what is unsaid in the story of Abkhazia? Will this be enough?

Eric

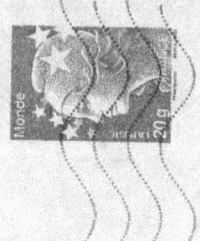

LA POSTE 255584

FRANCE 13-11-12

Maxim Gvinjia
Chamber of Commerce TPP
384900 Confederatov St. 37
Sukhum
République d'Abkhazie

By air mail
Par avion

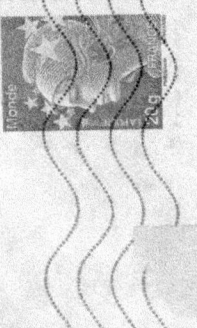

LA POSTE 26652A
FRANCE 15-11-12

Maxim Gvinjia
Chamber of Commerce TPP
384900 Confederatov St. 37
Sukhum
République d'Abkhazie

By air mail
Par avion

Paris, November 12th 2012

Dear Max,

Is this a story of the impossibility to live together after war, because of war?

Or does it have more to do with a question I wrote in a letter a few weeks ago: does the state include? Does it exclude?

Eric

Maxim Gvinjia
Chamber of Commerce TPP
384900 Confederatov St. 37
Sukhum
République d'Abkhazie

via Georgie

By air mail
Par avion

Paris, November 14th 2012

Dear Max,

Let's record some sounds today.

At the beach, in the forest, wherever you like.

Just sounds…

Eric

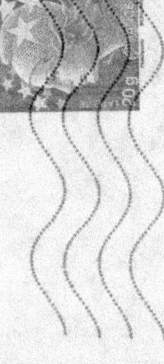

LA POSTE 256528A
FRANCE 19-11-12

Maxim Gvinjia
Chamber of Commerce TPP
384900 Confederatov St. 37
Sukhum
République d'Abkhazie

95076

Via GEORGIA

By air mail
Par avion

Paris, November 15th 2012

Dear Max,

Intermission. The midpoint of our film. Where do we go from here?

Eric

Maxim Gvinjia
Chamber of Commerce TPP
384900 Confederatov St. 37
Sukhum
République d'Abkhazie

GRUZIE

By air mail
Par avion

Paris, November 16th 2012

Dear Max,

August 26th 2008: a historic day.

Russia has just announced that it recognizes the independent state of Abkhazia. I am far away, on a ferryboat in Japan, and I see something on the television, but I can't understand what is being said. Where were you, Max? What were you doing?

Let's make some cinema!

Let's stage something again, let's re-enact August 26th 2008, the day Abkhazia was first recognized. I want you to set the stage for us. What happened on that day? Not in the world in general: in your life.

You woke up in the morning, where were you? At your house? What did you do? You drank coffee? You went to work? Where were you when Medvedev signed the decree of recognition? Take me through the events of your day, <u>everything</u>, hour to hour, from the moment you woke up, to the very end of the day. I want every detail.

Eric

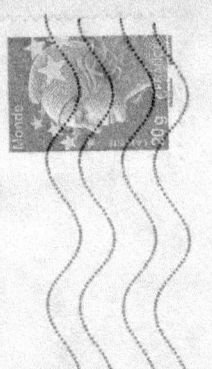

LA POSTE 25658A

FRANCE 23-11-12

Maxim Gvinjia
Chamber of Commerce TPP
384900 Confederatov St. 37
Sukhum
République d'Abkhazie

By air mail
Par avion

Paris, November 17th 2012

Dear Max,

We're going to re-film August 28th 2008 next time I visit you. Recreate every moment of that day. The film of Abkhazia on day one as a *recognized* nation. How should we proceed?

Eric

LA POSTE 25658A
FRANCE 25-11-12

Maxim Gvinjia
Chamber of Commerce TPP
384900 Confederatov St. 37
Sukhum
République d'Abkhazie

Via GEORG

By air mail
Par avion

Paris, November 20th 2012

Dear Max,

What did this change for you? Did being recognized make a difference?

Eric

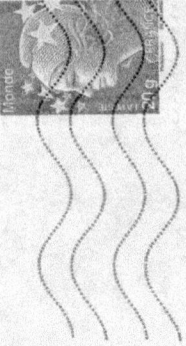

LA POSTE 25658A

FRANCE 26-11-12

Maxim Gvinjia
Chamber of Commerce TPP
384900 Confederatov St. 37
Sukhum
République d'Abkhazie

Via GEORGIA

By air mail
Par avion

Paris, November 21st 2012

Dear Max,

February 26th 2010. Another historic day. I am in Paris and Dov sends me an article announcing that Abkhazia has nominated a new Minister of Foreign Affairs: you.

Big day for Maxim Gvinjia?

Eric

LA POSTE   25558A
FRANCE   27-11-12

Maxim Gvinjia
Chamber of Commerce TPP
384900 Confederatov St. 37
Sukhum
République d'Abkhazie

Via ქართული

Paris, November 22nd 2012

Dear Max,

In the narration of a film, the day you become minister has to be a big moment in the script. A turning point in the story. How should we play it? How should we tell it? Can you give me a few variations on the theme of "Max becomes minister"?

Eric

POSTE 25558A
29-11-12

Maxim Gvinjia
...ber of Commerce TPP
... Confederatov St. 37
Sukhum
...blique d'Abkhazie

By air mail / Par avion

Post Office

UNDELIVERED / ONAFGELEWER / NON-DISTRIBUE
- UNKNOWN / ONBEKEND / INCONNU A CETTE ADRESSE
- NO SUCH NUMBER / NIE SO 'N NOMMER NIE / NUMERO N'EXISTE PAS
- NO SUCH STREET / NIE SO 'N STRAAT NIE / RUE N'EXISTE PAS
- ADDRESS INSUFFICIENT / ADRES ONVOLDOENDE / ADRESSE INCOMPLETE
- ADDRESS ILLEGIBLE / ADRES ONLEESBAAR / ADRESSE ILLISIBLE
- UNCLAIMED / ONAFGEHAAL / EN SOUFFRANCE
- REFUSED / GEWEIER / REFUSE
- BOX CLOSED / POSBUS GESLUIT / BOITE FERMEE
- GONE AWAY/NO ADDRESS LEFT / VERTREK - GEEN ADRES GELAAT NIE / PARTI SANS LAISSER D'ADRESSE

COMPLETED BY/VOLTOOI DEUR/COMPLETE PAR
NAME / NAAM / NOM

RETURN CHARGE PAYABLE / TERUGSENDKOSTE BETAALBAAR / FRAIS DE RETOUR PAYABLE

R
DATE / DATUM / DATE
NT 2463

LA POSTE   256588
FRANCE   30-11-12

Maxim Gvinjia
Chamber of Commerce TPP
384900 Confederatov St. 37
Sukhum
République d'Abkhazie

By air mail
Par avion

Paris, November 23rd 2012

Dear Max,

For a few years, while you were minister, we stopped exchanging emails. The news of your promotion to such an important function created a kind of distance. You didn't create that distance, but somehow the circumstances had become more solemn, and it didn't feel right to keep on the way we had before. What should I know about those years when we didn't speak?

Eric

LA POSTE 25558A
FRANCE 01-12-12

Maxim Gvinjia
Chamber of Commerce TPP
384900 Confederatov St. 37
Sukhum
République d'Abkhazie

By air mail
Par avion

Paris, November 24th 2012

Dear Max,

Are there things you couldn't talk about when you were minister?

Eric

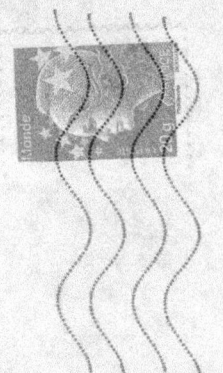

LA POSTE 25658A
FRANCE 04-12-12

Maxim Gvinjia
Chamber of Commerce TPP
384900 Confederatov St. 37
Sukhum
République d'Abkhazie

Georgia

By air mail
Par avion

Paris, November 29th 2012

Dear Max,

There are 193 countries in the United Nations, you need 97 votes to become a member state. How many do you have today? Will you ever get to 97? And what happens if you don't? What kind of future lies ahead?

Eric

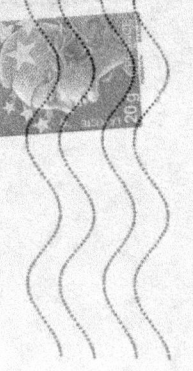

LA POSTE   25658A
FRANCE   05-12-12

Maxim Gvinjia
Chamber of Commerce TPP
384900 Confederatov St. 37
Sukhum
République d'Abkhazie

By air mail
Par avion

Paris, November 30th 2012

Dear Max,

Is there a freedom that comes with the idea that you are playing outside the rules of the game? That you, as a country, are a misfit? Living in a grey area, outside of the system of nations? A shadowy area *in between* states? Is there a space *in between* states?

Eric

LA POSTE   25658A

FRANCE   05-12-12

Maxim Gvinjia
Chamber of Commerce TPP
384900 Confederatov St. 37
Sukhum
République d'Abkhazie

GEORGIE

By air mail
Par avion

Paris, December 1ˢᵗ 2012

Dear Max,

Are you ever tempted to think in other terms than those of "national identity"? Did you ever feel that the very concept of the "nation state," which much of the world wants to deny you, should perhaps be ignored in favor of something else? A different idea of how to exist?

Eric

LA POSTE 25658A
FRANCE 10-12-12

Maxim Gvinjia
Chamber of Commerce TPP
384900 Confederatov St. 37
Sukhum
République d'Abkhazie

By air mail
Par avion

Paris, December 3rd 2012

Dear Max,

Some people say Abkhazia has escaped from Georgia but only to be eaten alive by Russia. What do you think? Will Abkhazia become the playground of Russian oligarchs?

Eric

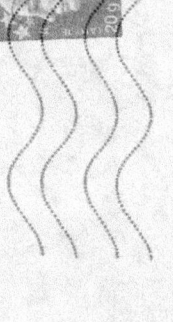

LA POSTE 25558A
FRANCE 11-12-12

Maxim Gvinjia
Chamber of Commerce TPP
384900 Confederatov St. 37
Sukhum
République d'Abkhazie

By air mail
Par avion

Paris, December 4th 2012

Dear Max,

What would be another future for Abkhazia?

Eric

LA POSTE 25552A

FRANCE 14-12-12

Maxim Gvinjia
Chamber of Commerce TPP
384900 Confederatov St. 37
Sukhum
République d'Abkhazie

GEORGIA

By air mail
Par avion

Paris, December 6th 2012

Dear Max,

Are there things I didn't ask about but should have asked you about?

Eric

LA POSTE   256658A
FRANCE   15-12-12

Maxim Gvinjia
Chamber of Commerce TPP
384900 Confederatov St. 37
Sukhum
République d'Abkhazie

By air mail
Par avion

Paris, December 7th 2012

Dear Max,

Now you are back to civilian life. What happened? Are you done with politics?

Eric

Maxim Gvinjia
Chamber of Commerce TPP
384900 Confederatov St. 37
Sukhum
République d'Abkhazie

By air mail
Par avion

Paris, December 8th 2012

Dear Max,

Are you happy? Are you ever sad?

Eric

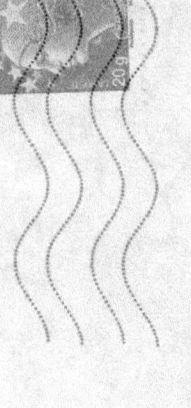

LA POSTE 25652A

FRANCE 19-12-12

Maxim Gvinjia
Chamber of Commerce TPP
384900 Confederatov St. 37
Sukhum
République d'Abkhazie

By air mail
Par avion

Paris, December 10th 2012

Dear Max,

What will you be doing a year from today? Tell me about that day a year from now?

Eric

LA POSTE 25668A
FRANCE 20-12-12

Maxim Gvinjia
Chamber of Commerce TPP
384900 Confederatov St. 37
Sukhum
République d'Abkhazie

georgia

By air mail
Par avion

Paris, December 11th 2012

Dear Max,

I must tell you something: when I sent you that first letter from Paris, back in June, the thought that it would arrive wasn't in the realm of the possible for me. In a way, I didn't really write it for you, I expected to see it come back to my studio with a stamp on the envelope from the French post office saying "Return to sender / country doesn't exist." I just wanted to see what the post-office would say upon returning an impossible letter. But apparently the impossible is possible.

A few weeks ago, when I was mailing one the many letters that would follow, a man standing next to the mailbox caught a glimpse of the address on the envelope. He asked me what I was doing. I told him I was sending a letter to Abkhazia. He asked me what that was. So I told him. And I told him about you, and I told him about the film we are making. The man smiled. I could tell he didn't believe a word I was telling him, but I could also tell that he liked the story.

Did you ever really receive my letters, Max?

Eric

Published by Bergen Kunsthall and Poulet-Malassis
on the occasion of the exhibition:
Eric Baudelaire "The Secession Sessions"
Bergen Kunsthall, NO.5
17 January – 16 February 2014

The exhibition is a co-production of
Bergen Kunsthall; Bétonsalon – Center of art
and research and UC Berkeley Art Museum and
Pacific Film Archive (BAM/PFA). In partnership
with Kadist Art Foundation.

Editor:
Eric Baudelaire

Design:
Marie Proyart and Mathieu Bernardis

Printing:
lulu.com

This second edition includes an additional letter
dated 13 November 2012, returned by mail
on 12 March 2015.

Copyright:
Catalogue © Bergen Kunsthall and Poulet-Malassis
Texts © The author
Images © The artist

ISBN 978-82-93101-16-1

Bergen Kunsthall
Rasmus Meyers allé 5, N-5015 Bergen, Norway
www.kunsthall.no

Poulet-Malassis
Éditeur – Producteur
41bis Quai de la Loire, A304, 75019 Paris, France
www.pouletmalassis.com

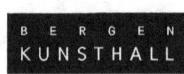 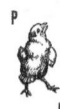